Those Summer–Soothing Days

David Jaffin

Those Summer-Soothing Days

*The books by Dr. David Jaffin are housed
by the special collections
of New York University's libraries*

First published in the United Kingdom in 2024 by
Shearsman Books
PO Box 4239
Swindon
SN3 9FN

Shearsman Books Ltd Registered Office
30–31 St. James Place, Mangotsfield, Bristol BS16 9JB
(this address not for correspondence)

www.shearsman.com

ISBN 978-1-84861-865-7

Production, composition, & cover design: Edition Wortschatz,
a service of Neufeld Verlag, Neudorf bei Luhe/Germany
E-Mail info@edition-wortschatz.de, www.edition-wortschatz.de

Title illustration:
Claude Monet (1840–1926), *Woman Seated under the Willows*, 1880,
National Gallery of Art, Washington
(Everett Collection/Shutterstock.com)

Printed in Germany

Contents

7

With continuing thanks for
Marina Moisel
preparing
this manuscript

and to Hanni Bäumler
for her well-placed
photograph

If I had to classify my poetry, it could best be done through the classical known "saying the most by using the least". The aim is thereby set: transparency, clarity, word-purity. Every word must carry its weight in the line and the ultimate aim is a unity of sound, sense, image and idea. Poetry, more than any other art, should seek for a unity of the senses, as the French Symbolists, the first poetic modernists, realized through the interchangeability of the senses: "I could hear the colors of her dress." One doesn't hear colors, but nevertheless there is a sensual truth in such an expression.

Essential is "saying the most by using the least". Compression is of the essence. And here are some of my most personal means of doing so turning verbs into nouns and the reverse, even within a double-context "Why do the leaves her so ungenerously behind". Breaking words into two or even three parts to enable both compression and the continuing flow of meaning. Those words must be placed back together again, thereby revealing their inner structure-atomising.

One of my critics rightly said: "Jaffin's poetry is everywhere from one seemingly unrelated poem to the next." Why? Firstly because of my education and interests trained at New York University as a cultural and intellectual historian. My doctoral dissertation on historiography emphasizes the necessary historical continuity. Today we often judge the past with the mind and mood of the present, totally contrary to their own historical context. I don't deny the past-romanticism and classical but integrate them within a singular modern context of word-usage and sensibility. Musically that would place me within the "classical-romantic tradition" of Haydn, Mozart, Mendelssohn, Brahms and Nielsen but at the very modern end of that tradition.

My life historically is certainly exceptional. My father was a prominent New York Jewish lawyer. The law never interested me, but history always did. A career as a cultural-intellectual historian was mine-for-the-asking, but I rejected historical relativism. That led me to a marriage with a devout German lady – so I took to a calling of Jesus-the-Jew in post-Auschwitz Germany. For ca. two decades I wrote and lectured all over Germany on Jesus the Jew. Thereby my knowledge and understanding of both interlocked religions became an essential part of my being. History, faith and religion two sides of me but also art, classical music and literature were of essential meaning – so many poems on poetry, classical music and painting.

Then Rosemarie and I have been very happily married for 62 years now. Impossible that a German and Jew could be so happily married so shortly after the war? I've written love poems for her, hundreds and hundreds over those 62 years, not only the love poems, as most are, of the first and often unfulfilling passion, but "love and marriage go together like a horse and carriage". Perhaps too prosaic for many poets?

When did I become a poet? My sister Lois wrote reasonably good poetry as an adolescent. I, only interested in sports until my Bar Mitzvah, a tournament tennis and table-tennis player, coached baseball and basketball teams, also soccer.

My sister asked whether I'd ever read Dostoyevsky. I'd only read John R. Tunis sports books and the sports section of the *New York Times* so I answered "in which sports was he active?" She said, rather condescendingly, "If you haven't read Dostoyevsky, you haven't lived." So I went to the library for the very first time and asked for a book by this Dostoyevsky. I received *Poor People*, his first book, that made him world famous. My mother shocked to see me reading and most especially a book about poor people said, "David, don't read that it will make you sad, unhappy – we, living in Scarsdale, weren't after all, poor people. From there it went quickly to my Tolstoy, Hardy and so on. In music it started with the hit parade, then *Lost in the Stars*, then the popular classics and with 15 or 16 my Haydn, Mozart, Schütz, Victoria ... And then at Ann Arbor and NYU to my artists, most especially Giovanni Bellini, Van der Weyden, Georges de la Tour, Corot and Gauguin ...

But it was Wallace Stevens' reading in the early 50s in the YMHA that set me off – he didn't read very well, but his 13 Ways of Looking at a Blackbird, Idea of Order at Key West, Two Letters (in *Poems Posthumous*), Peter Quince at the Clavier, The Snowman ... and the excellent obituary in *Time* magazine plus the letter he answered some of my poems with compliments but "you must be your own hardest critic". That pre-determined my extremely self-critical way with a poem. Please don't believe that prolific means sloppy, for I'm extremely meticulous with each and every poem.

My poems were published in the order written and I'm way ahead of any counting… The poem is a dialogical process as everything in life. The words come to me not from me, and if they strike or possibly join-a-union then I become desperate, read long-winded poets like Paz to set me off – he's very good at odd times. Those poems need my critical mood-mind as much as I need their very specially chosen words – not the "magic words" of the romantics, but the cleansed words of Jaffin – Racine used only 500 words. My words too are a specially limited society, often used, but in newly-felt contexts.

O something very special: I have a terrible poetic memory. If I had a good one as presumably most poets, I'd write say one poem about a butterfly, and every time I see/saw a butterfly it would be that one, that poem. But I forget my poems, so each butterfly, lizard, squirrel… is other-placed, other-mooded, other-worded, other-Jaffined. That's the main reason why I am most certainly the most prolific of all poets.

Shakespeare is the greatest of us: his sonnets live most from the fluency and density of his language. I advise all future poets to keep away from his influence and the poetic greatness of The Bible.

Yours truly
David Jaffin

P. S.: As a preacher the truth (Christ) should become straight-lined, timelessly so, but as a poet it's quite different. What interests me most are those contradictions which live deeply within all of us, not only in theory, but daily in the practice. And then the romantics have led me to those off-sided thoroughly poetic truths that mysteriously not knowing where that darkened path will lead us.

*"A foolish consistency is
the hobgoblin of little minds"*

(Emerson)

This early (2)

> *a) morning summer*

> day had be

> come so quiet
> that one could

> almost hear

> *b) that silence*

> breathing
> the flower

> s in to their
> colored awaken

> ings.

Only after

wards did he
realise that

summer night'
s refreshing

coolness had
called the

distant moon
in to its

quietly reveal
ing composure.

She put-

on such a
sun-bright

ravishing
smile that I

almost felt ex
tinguished

by its inten
sing effect.

She was (12)

a) that kind of

person who

could sudden
ly react emot

b) ionally to

what would seem

for many as a
trivial theme

whether for

c) example a parti

cular brand of
sparkling wa

ter should be
boycotted be

cause of this

d) or that environ

mental reason After
feeling our way

to a common re
sponse we fin

ally settled on

e) the tap-water

theme of time-
selectivity

in our aging
years leaving Rose

marie and myself re

f) lieved that after

noon had passed
without major

discords on re
latively minor

g) themes what con

tinually remain

ed difficult our
diverging taste

on art and art
ists I tried

h) with Redon on

flowers and Con

stable on cloud
s though she

countered with

i) that hasty-brush

ed Corinth all-
of-which-remain

ed dead-ended
false-starter

j) s Though our

taste on music

could remain
quite change

ably dependent
on how it's in

k) terpreted and

our own and its

preparation
for an adequate

response it still

l) remains the same

music wanting to
be received as

a friend on–its–
own–term

s.

Pastoral *(6)*

a) themes accompan

ied good poetry

for many centur
ies for some

b) as an antidote

to the manner

ed appearance
s of court life

and/or the cit
id oft unpoet

c) ic raison d'

être But now

it could e
asily reestab

d) lish itself in

its end–time

dying-out last
phase Reading

the current

e) plentitude of

books and maga
zine article

s on bees
still doesn't

replenish

f) their dying-out

for the prett
ily expectant

flowering duly-
scented respon

se.

If you don' (3)

a) t listen to

really good

music as if
for the first

b) time and dia

logue each a

waiting paint
ing down to its

depthed–exposure

c) s then daily

life too will
remain for you

as a routine
ever–so–much.

It's often (4)

a) *the negative*

examples that

predetermine
and even

b) *motivate*

our own

future-calling
s For some

an imitation

c) *of a good*

teacher's way
s and mean

s but more
like a bad

d) *teacher's*

"I don't want

to make those
same insensit

ive mistake
s."

Common sense (4)

a) seems uncommon

ly rare these

days of out-
placed superla

b) tive languag

ings while lack

ing Mark Twain'
s healthy earth-

bound frog-jump

c) ing hyperbole

s The center
has fallen-off

not only polit
ically but in

d) daily upgraded

eye-sensing

expectation
s.

With those (3)

a) 2nd World War'

s mass-shoot

ings of Jew
s they shot

b) their own con

science and

previously
prevailing

humanity

c) to their dead-

bound irretriev
ably-buried

no-escape-
routes-left.

Mood-felt (4)

a) poems as those

most cherish

ed landscape
s of Constable

and Corot leave

b) one feeling a

part of that
inescapable

time-receding
expressive

c) ness while

this warmthed

summer seem
s more and

more as if sus
pending in a

d) rain-sun cy

cle of repetit

ive transpar
ence

s.

Half way mea

sures may stim
ulate the need

for future com
promises or

they may a
waken perhap

s from both
sides an im

pending desire
for more.

Long unpaint *(3)*

a) ed houses may

mirror owner

s more inclined
for inside

b) pleasures and/

or ones not

too obsessive
ly concerned

with outside
appearance

c) and/or

with fewer hidd

en secrets to
be carefully

painted-over.

Big flower

s remind me
of that kind

of woman
usually scent

ed for a dis
tant expressive

ness.

Retired teach (2)

a) ers may quite

unconscious

ly continue
practicing

though no
longer profess

b) ionally espec

ially when their

husbands re
main within teach

able range.

Parents rare *(3)*

a) ly realise

how to take

the right tone
with their

b) grown-up

children re

main children
for them and

parents usual

c) ly miss-the-

boat for an e
ven-levelled

commonly-de
sired route.

He'd become (4)

a) that comfortab

ly retired pro

fessional Eng
lish-type Ameri

b) can with his

personally

wood-bespoken
indwelling

library and an
open fire for

c) remembrance-

sake now re

laxing in that
comfortable

feeling of a

d) job and (e

ven with a
touch of self–

ironic modesty a
life more than

less well–done.

Indirect way (6)

a) s of reaching

one's cherish

ed goals open
ing-up newly

b) sourced route

s as the daught

er-in-law
rather than

through a dir

c) ect confrontat

ion with
one's not yet

thoroughly e
mancipated son

d) Or George's way

of solving medi

cal problem
s That's why di

plomatic means re

e) main the best

way of solving
difficult prob

lems whereas
war as the First

f) World War leaves

its accumulat

ing debris to
help the second

one in its still
unresolving cause.

Poor but out

played Europe

as once Poland
caught between

contending pow
ers poised and

ready to dimin
ish its already

wearing credibil
ity.

It's warming- *(3)*

a) up-again as

if in personal

response to
my own increas

b) ingly sourced-

creativity

Does nature
mirror our own

state-of-being

c) or are we but

the shadowing
image of its

self-declar
ing certain

ty.

Not even (3)

a) these careful

ly orchestrat

ed gardened–
flowers and the

b) quietly contem

plative amass

ing of heaven
ly clouds could

ease the uncer
tainties of a

c) world off-course

immensed in in

escapable impend
ing darkness

es.

Raphael our (4)

a) retarded son

now in his

mid–50s sudden
ly became dead

b) ly afraid of

whatever wasn'

t familiar
to him It was

as if the

c) world could only

be trusted if
it had been

sensed touched
and seen as if

d) the outside

world remained

foreign and
dangerous.

He kept writ *(3)*

a) ing day after

day to prove

that the poet
(that other

b) side of self)

was still pre

pared to dia
logue its most

necessary

c) still untold ex

pressiveness
with such an

otherwise
self-person.

What remain (2)

a) ed sacred for

his always quest

ioning mind-
sense only what

that one God
Jesus of Nazar

b) eth and His

book bequested

through The
Father claimed

as its own
sacredly-held

domain.

This morning

slowly became
silently lift

ed from the
realms of an

all-encompass
ing darkness.

Those horse

s standing as
leep to a stat

uesque poise of
timely-evoking

dreamed–awaken
ings.

Left-over

s generally re
ferred to what

tasted better
the day before

but it's also
a disagreement

warmed–up for
continuing

distraction
s.

Mozart's Don (5)

a) *Giovanni as most*

operas musical

led to an in
substantial re

b) *petitive and*

superficial

text compared
with his master

ly singspiel

c) *The Magic Flute*

where Mozart'
s existential

faith receive
s the onflowing

d) depth of his

best operatic

indulgence
s so varied

space and sound

e) ed to a most

convincing
word–wise and

musical one
ness.

He spoke of (11)

a) fully loving

his life–long

wife and daily
companion

while still un
able to divert

b) his too oft

uprising eye

s at the command
ing sight of o

therwise beauti

c) fully-form

ed women We
all must learn-

to-live with
known or e

d) ven lesser

realized ten

sions that
two-direction

us to an oft

e) permanent un

ease of an in
wardly divid

ed self My
mother's favor

f) ite "Variety'

s the spice of

life" may taste
fully contrary

to her every

g) Monday's lamb

chops every Tues
day's chicken …

but it shouldn'
t direction us

h) to where as

my father would

have said "our
defenses have

become most
vulnerable"

i) What's last

said doesn't

necessarily
imply a final

ly realized

j) raison d'être

Mozart's Magic Flute
and his Requiem

two swan–song
s poised at op

k) posite personal

and theological

ly unresolving dir
ection

s.

When his (2)

> *a) thought-poem*
>
> s begin to
>
> take-on a
> moralizing
>
> tone then the
> pulpit's again
>
>
> *b) on a high-rise*
>
> level and the
>
> poet's become
> more or less
>
> a self-inhabit
> ing parishion
>
> er.

Reading (3)

a) past-publish

able poems
enables me to

b) conceive more

of a differ

ently-samed
start – begin

at the possi

c) ble end of

those inevit
ably sloping

poetic silen
ces.

When repeat

ed poetry-tires-
me-out no re

treat left ex
cept a withdraw

al in to what'
s not relev

antly self-ap
parent.

Our summer (2)

a) gardened me

in so various

direction
s that it be

came difficult
to center a

b) most personal

obliging

though inward
ly contrast

ing unity.

Bees in their

domesticat
ing wandering

s remind me
of my Swab

ian friend
s landscaped

to person a
need for just–

so timed–re
lease.

This garden' *(2)*

a) s been so butter

flied with change

able coloring
s that even in

my most suit

b) able reclining

armchair I be
gin to flutter

as well unex
pected imagin

ings.

Are these

    birds (one-ton
    ed song) not

    really music
    ally adept

    but more a
    life-pulsing

    continuity.

Do these so

    brightly dis
    tinguishing

    summer time
    s remain never

    theless incap
    able of a

    solemn
    time–encompass

    ing express
    iveness.

Are the less *(3)*

a) er finely craft

ed composer

s of the Haydn–
era however de

b) pendent on

their so in

dependent
master still

a times ori

c) ginally voic

ed in their
own most per

sonal way
s.

Taking a dis (2)

a) tance to my

own thought-re

flection
s these cotton-

like insubstan
tial cloud

b) s hardly as

sembling for

a steadfast
ly certained

continuity.

A light

breeze skin-
touched an a

wakening need
for this time-

flowing garden
ed pleasur

ings.

Hortensia (2)

a) as self-assum

ing as the

name would im
ply extrava

gantly express

b) ive more than

touched with a

self-reclaim
ing sense of

flowered–super
iority.

A short even (6)

a) ing of spirit

ual motets

from Josquin
to the present

b) purifying the

word as with

Schütz to its
own self-pro

claiming in

c) tent or as

with Mendels
sohn just right

ly modulating
for angelic

interlude

d) s Bach may have

been the High
Baroque culmin

ation of relig
ious music but

the motet they

e) sang perhaps

too self-con
sciously involv

ed of such an
intricate coun

terpunctual

f) excursions re

minding more of
earlier Flemish

master
s.

Reading back *(3)*

a) the three-year

s-ago Jaffin

Opus 40 seem
s little differ

b) ent from what

I'm now writ

ing if any
thing with

those thousand
s of poems bet

c) ween perhaps an

extended length

of theme and
variation'

s expressive
ness.

I sensed (2)

> *a) danger the way*

wild animal

s do Indian-
like wind pre

determining
a close friend

> *b) with a 40-*

years-younger

woman and his
long-time

wife also some
how vacantly

present.

Does that (4)

a) *heavily furr*

ed highly

suspicious
cat come daily

b) *here oft sitt*

ing quite home

ly at our
front-door step

s implying I'

c) *m your cat*

which I've
time and a

gain guarant
eed just isn'

d) *t so If you'*

d just

listen loud
ly enough.

Dream-length *(2)*

a) s seem lesser-

sensed than

this pre-deter
mining open

sky's view

b) though they do

remain closer
aware of an

otherwise
time-space

affinity.

Catullus *(3)*

a) the Roman pro-

type of a

modern poet
couldn't free

b) himself from

the fanged poi

son-snake in
stincts of his

promiscuous
ly so-called

c) loved-one

who'd stung

him right to
his heart'

s eternal rhy
thm.

Starting this (4)

a) brightly-attuned

early July day
with a soft

b) ly compelling

kissed the whole

of Rosemarie'
s very-being the

whiteness of
her fully bod

c) ied awakening

s to my daily

lip's time-as
serting reapprais

als of such a
beautifying

d) woman at her

age still deny

ing time's u
sually author

ised identify
ing-source.

As most al

ways these dream
s have taken

their own time-e
clipsing rout

ed to what
could-have-been

otherwise but
nevertheless

self-intention
ed.

That tiny (2)

a) bird almost

as an after

thought colored
to my own self-

contentment

b) branched an in

terlude of its
flighty self-

finding where
about

s.

Can one *(3)*

a) leave one'

s own self-i

dentifying
raison d'

b) être behind

as these mi

grants to a
new beginn

ing of thor
oughly unsour

c) ced yet al

ways present

ly time-with
holding expect

ation
s.

It's the *(3)*

a) continual

feel of a new

ly published
book

b) that leave

s my search

ing hands and
fully sourced

sensual aware

c) ness to its

own self-pur
posing irre

trievable
appreciat

ions.

Do histori *(2)*

a) cal places e

ven those once

bombed to a
self–retriev

ing past bring
the all of

b) their long

history for

the observer'
s self–attun

ed appreciat
ions.

Learning a (3)

a) foreign language

one of the

best mean
s of re-dis

b) covering your

own too easily

accustomed
to its daily

use to what
we never should

c) take-for-grant

ed the word-

spell of Shakes
peare's mono

logues for ex
ample.

If man's be (2)

a) come but a Kafka

esque self-sha

dowing image
of his very-be

ing because
he's lost that

b) hold on what

The Good Lord

created for us
to sanctify

His own self-
fulfilling

poetic-be
ing.

A private (2)

a) garden recept

ively self-en

closing the in
timacy of its

flowering re
newal domesti

b) cated but still

coloring its

self-appreciat
ive's time-shar

ings.

Communist (5)

a) German must be
translated
from its wall
ed-in other

b) wiseness One
people's scarce
ly unified
to become di
vided once a

c) gain from its
linguistic
ground-base
I'd become traum
atised too as

d) a migrant in a

strange lang

uage distant
land needing to

become recultur
ed to a foreign

e) people's other

wise cultural

religious and
most especial

ly political
past.

1492 *(3)*

a) *Spain final*

ly unified but
at the cost

of its Judaic-
Moslemic multi-

b) *cultural trad*

ition and to a

workless ethic
of a less sover

eignly holding
ground-base

c) *Its always sun*

ful empire slow

ly descending
in to a Europ

ean-sourced ir
relevance.

Does this (4)

a) July rain re

member its

own last-tim
ed purifying

b) of a land

dried to its

bottom-down
time-inhabit

ing ground-
base This rain

c) seems to be

rhymed to a

pre-determin
ing time-spell

as if called
without reali

d) sing why as

with Gerhard

Richter's chanc
ed-occasion

s.

"Unequalled (5)

　　a) Marriage" oft

　　as with Cranach

　　and Leibl as a
　　measure of their

　　b) still activat

　　ing manliness

　　though for the
　　young women

　　involved the

　　c) hidden purse

　　that's become
　　equally activat

　　ed as well
　　for dead-time

d) future pleasur

able enjoyment

s Neither sex
nor money seem

to have lost

e) their timeless-

hold on our
lower-level

Baal–appeal
ings.

Are gifted (2)

a) *poets writing*

all-along as

a defense a
gainst those

indefinable
claims of a

b) *continually*

oncoming death

The graveyard
has imaged its

own share of
life-living

poetry.

Lost identi *(3)*

a) ties become

as difficult

to obtain once
again for a

b) time-intend

ing cause as

those seldom
first–time

old–age friend
ships that

c) seem to e

lude their most

necessary
time–extend

ing hold.

Ease and com (3)

a) fort seem to

encompass

the inescap
able claim

b) s of an a

ging society

But it's just
the opposite

a newly dis
covered calling

c) of whatever

kind or mode

that keeps us
(at least tempor

arily) young
and fit.

We certain *(5)*

a) ly don't chose

our children

(a lesson
which my par

ents learned

b) the hard way)

Nor do we
choose our par

ents Uncle Ir
ving would

c) have been an

ideal father

for me (or so
I imagine)

and his flashy

d) then suicidal

son Moss Andrew
would perhap

s have worked-
well with my

e) also always-on-

the-move money-

oriented fa
ther.

I'm complete *(5)*

a) ly dependent

on good poetry

translation
s from an un

b) learned foreign

language while

"understand
ing" takes-on

its most essen

c) tial meaning

If it's only
the mind's–

length then
it should be

d) come word for

word line for

line But if
"understand

ing" encompass
es all of the

e) senses as well

being freed

while poetical
ly self–recall

ing.

Watches *(3)*

a) may encompass

time down to

its very second–
hand precision

b) Yet we live

with the illus

ion that time
itself has be

come the hand–
maiden of our

c) inordinate

claims on its

steadfast
ly reliable

very-being.

Shostako (6)

a) vich's 8th Quar

tet may have-

been for
him both a

very personal

b) elegiac summing-

up of his creat

ive expressive
ness and a memor

ial for the

c) millions of dead

especially Russ
ians at the

hands of Hitler'
s death-invoking

d) henchmen But for

me it displayed

two very contrast
ing aspects of

his complex musi

e) cality the al

most classical
depth of his

best slow move
ments and the

f) barbaric inten

sity of his

defense of
personal and

political free
dom.

Glazunov' (4)

a) s 6th Quartet'

s hard-to-

place within a
Russian until

then under-
nourished quartet-

b) context though

perhaps within
the transition

al even more
individual way

s of Nielsen and

c) Sibelius of De

bussy and Ravel
The sliding theme

of its first
movement made me

feel once again

d) that long-ago

water-slide in
to Lake Champlain'

s receptive-cool
ness.

The sound

less reach of
these expans

ive tree
s has left me

mirroring re
flective time–

sensed imagin
ings.

In Thai

land 13 youth
s in the depth

s of a watering
cave's deadly in

stinctual dark
ness awaiting

help that may
never survive

them.

When moved *(2)*

a) by Constable'

s landscaping

as any other
tree alive to

its natural
purposing in

b) the midst

of 200 year

s of a time-
escaping

now and no-
where else.

To become too *(3)*

a) taken with one'

s own voice

(as I remember
his warming-

b) ups for a

church-recept

ive audience)
is like often

mirroring

c) for a self-

satisfying
if hardly last

ing impressive
ness.

These Satur

day morning
summer-like

clouds open
ing to an un

known though
spacious

ly self-reveal
ing beyond

ness.

At each anniver (2)

a) sary Neil in

scribes a new

poem for his
long-loved

wife especial

b) ly reminding

their marriage
had been seal

ed for still
unopening pleas

ures.

I asked a (11)

a) young Polish

lady if Chopin

was a truly
Polish composer

b) and received

the usual expect

ant–answer but
if he was why

then no real

c) successor

s and if he
was why have

the French re
claimed his spec

d) ially finely

touching sensi

bility though
Polish he felt

himself to be

e) the more of

his doubly-
sourced iden

tity Was Wein
berg then a

f) Polish composer

born and bred

in Warsaw even
at first influen

ced by the Polish
late romantic

g) tradition

But his Polish

family totally
wiped-out as

most other Jew

h) ish familie

s and then
strongly influen

ced by his very-
Russian mentor

i) Shostakovich

I personal

ly doubt whether
this Jewish–Russ

ian composer

j) still inhabit

ed by a spec
ially Polish rais

on d'être And
I my-other-self

k) sourced if any

where else than

in a Jewish–German
poetic trad

ition.

Once again (3)

a) that fully-furr

ed cat expect

antly waiting
(for what?)

b) at my door-

step with a

sense of possess
ive ownership

in her space-

c) accommodating

eyes Have I de
prived her of

a most necess
ary identity-

cause.

Last day be (4)

a) *fore our summer-*

time Italian

ate vacation
Can a daily

b) *poetic writer*

realise a time'

s-off when his
eyes stop see

ing through

c) *to those dia*

loguing imperson
ed objects

and when his
mind's dulled

from thinking-

d) *things-out to*

a finalized if
at times self–

contradict
ory end.

That young (2)

a) lady across

the window

ed–length of
her half–dress

ed accommodat

b) ing look

ing right
and left of

my word–ab
sorbing eye

s.

When poetry (2)

a) seems to have

gone astray

neither here
nor there

but as an un

b) leashed dog

random–path
ed to its own

celebrating
half-instinct

ual complian
ce.

That out-

looking window'
s darkened

now as if
newly perspect

ived to an un
familiar yet

neverthe
less self-con

fining cause.

Are these

wettened though
sun-purposing

leaves but a
wind-hesitant

reminder of
what's holding-

fast to a still
undefinable

cause.

Chestnut (2)

a) s though hard-

shelled open

ing their im
permanent

ly expectant-

b) self to the

soft taste of
time-consum

ing desira
bilitie

s.

He became *(3)*

a) so self-import

ant as a Humpty

Dumpty situat
ing his most

b) sanctioned

and superior

presence until
that great fall

left him unpiece

c) ably untogether

ed irreparab
ly time-for

saken.

The German *(4)*

a) s after two

lost world war

s living now in
a thoroughly

b) unheroic world

where Mozart'

s by far the
favored compos

er no longer
the heroic Beet

c) hoven Other coun

tries as Israel

life-dependent
on an heroic

ethos when sur

d) vival looms

higher than any
other important

though part–time
commitment.

Pure or engaged (4)

(poetry to the memory of Jorge Guillén)

a) Pure poetry

is the most

engaged of all
reordering and

beautifying

b) a world in com

plete disarray
when man's be

come his own
worst enemy

c) now purified

to a newly sens

ed beauty in
the lasting

and lesser i

d) mage of our

own Creator'
s raison d'

être.

Such an in (2)

a) timate person

al tone in

her child–like
voice as if

meeting in her
young daughter'

b) s curious re

ceptivity the

mirror to her
own once hav

ing been
so young.

These celest

ial clouds immen
sing ever so

slowly a time-
encompassing

procession
al.

What "Christ (3)

a) would have done"

is hardly a

question for
human consider

b) ation because

he mostly chose

to what
might seem con

trary to our

c) best enlighten

ed humanely
pharisaic con

sideration
s.

Here in Eur *(2)*

a) ope it's hard

to discover a

place untouch
ed by Jewish

suffering
most especial

b) ly if you're

scented for

blood-sourced
ground-based

remembran
ces.

If green' (2)

> *a) s the color of*
>
> life's intended
>
> purposings and
> I'm 90 % green-
>
> blind does that

> *b) imply I've only*
>
> a 10 % hold on
> life's depth–
>
> compelling
> susceptibli
>
> ties.

Even she too

> one of his
> most avid poet
>
> ic admirer
> s held–him–
>
> up to her own
> specialized
>
> self-confirm
> ing sensibilit
>
> ies.

Are the hea *(2)*

a) vens too mov

ing with these

cloud's irre
trievable

time-search
ing reach or

b) does that static

blue remain

as a stead
fast guarantee

of an immov
able self-cer

tainty.

I've been (2)

a) gardened once a

gain with a

fullness of
flowering

familiar

b) ity that color

s me just as
they would

have it time
ly self-encom

passing.

Can a nation (2)

    a) so divided

    so long as

    Poland develop
    an indigenous

    culture all-its-

    b) own or are Chopin

    and Weinberg its
    greatest composer

    s also inhabit
    ing a cultural-

    divide.

Hardly a day (2)

a) lost for those

unspoken poem

s continual
ly demanding

a voice of
their own Each

b) poem sourced

to its individ

ually birthed
and found necess

ary time-ex

posure
s.

Snails hous (2)

a) ed in a pervad

ing stillness

as slowly kept
as their drawn-

down phrasing
s though daily

b) tasting of the

fullness of

this summer'
s ever-ripen

ing sumptu
ous green'

s.

These South

Tyrolean hill
s have been

climbing-me-
up just as

far as my
eyes can real

ise their new
ly establish

ing claim
s.

Threaten

ing cloud
s amassed as an

invading army
overwhelming

even the hea
ven's timeless

ly invoking
assurance

s.

That sweet (2)

a) child encircled

by the loving

embraces of two
rather late

middle-aged
corpulent

b) ladies could e

asily have been

taken for an
early renaiss

ance Italian
ate Jesus.

Summer 1946

the 9–year–old
Jaffin had fin

ally talked–him
self out Our

counsellor Ray
Poggenburg not

knowing I wasn'
t asleep to a

fellow counsell
or "My girl

friend doesn'
t know I'm

Jewish should
I tell her At

that moment and
at none other

did I first
become a Jew.

Our Bressanone (2)

a) hotel richly gar

dened in the

midst of that
Medieval town

surrounded
by those immen

b) sing mountain

s made me feel

how small and
even shallow

I'd be
come.

Far away (2)

a) *thoughts may*

have been

origined here
where distan

ces seem to

b) *be accommodat*

ing one's mo
mentary self-

purposing de
sign

s.

Butterflie

s fluttering
me about until

they're smooth
ly landed in

the softness
of their read

ily time-accomm
odating leave

s.

The scent (2)

a) of this new

ly-cut and

closely-cho
sen grass a

wakening
the appeal

b) s of some

long past and

yet mutely
responding

remembran
ce.

I wouldn't (3)

a) have wanted to

be Jewed here

in this re
mote and her

b) oically in

spired German

ic landscap
ing but rather

to have be
come a part of

c) its musically

and poetic al

ly early awaken
ing sensibil

ity.

It all went *(2)*

a) on behind-the-

scenes she

managed it
that way slow

ly isolating
her gifted hus

b) band and two

unprotected

children to
the extensive

claws of her
sickening

out-reach.

A stealthy *(2)*

a) cat creeping

along this gar

den's wall pro
tected instinct

ively enclos

b) ing but never-

the-less not
so harmless

ly shadowing
illusion

s.

As a child (2)

a) I thought those

wearing eye-

glasses had be
come especial

ly gifted but
only now real

b) lise the imag

inings of a

timely-perspect
ive appear

ance.

Now soccer-

success is be
coming more and

more the mea
sure of a nat

ion's self-re
assuring qual

ity not real
ly different

than the sport'
s ability of

an American
youth.

Rosemarie (2)

a) in her 80's now

sunning her

self after a
pleasurable

afternoon
swim neither

b) more nor less

ingratiat

ing as when
we honey-moon

ed not-far-
from-here some

57 years ago.

I've become

daily so in
creasingly

poemed that
I may most

unsuspect
ingly be slow

ly merged in
to a unified

self-person.

If a poem'

    s not able
    to breathe

    it will soon
    become deadly

    inert and its
    rhythmic-pulse

    will dry-down
    to echoless-

    silence
    s.

A sole bird

    repetitively
    chirping some

    unanswered
    message or per

    haps rhymed to
    its self-ex

    ploring iden
    tity-source.

It's the (3)

a) same accustom

ed view a

cross the lake
to Desenzano

b) but it seem

s to be view

ing me other
wise as if

in all these
years it hadn'

c) t become a

ware of my

yearly desire
to explore its

self-conceal
ing past.

It's her (4)

a) *home-hotel*

or her child

hood–self
she knows non

b) *other except*

the impersonal

coming and go
ing of strang

ers and their

c) *oft strange*

ly foreign
tongues and yet

it remains per
sonally her

d) *no other*

wise sense of

being safely
parented here.

Sperling (6)

a) was a spy

we all knew

that behind
the German line

s and then a

b) gainst the

Russian Commun
ists he died

suddenly knock
ed-down by a

c) foreign car

on 5th Avenue

He was one-
and-for-all

in love with

d) his best friend'

s wife They
all–knew–that

immortalized
by his pro

e) found 3rd gener

ation unintell

ectualised
knowledge of

f) the great and

lesser master'

s brush–stroke
s.

Sirmione (3)

a) This soft

Italian
ate summer morn

ing seems to
have just been

b) breezed-in

with that mount

ain-surround
ing-spacious

ness securing

c) a permanent

hold on its
time-depth

ed-distancing
s.

Her self-ap *(2)*

a) parent pretti

ness blemish

ed by a manner
ed even half–

closed–eyed
estrange

b) d expression

of has she

been touched
too early too

young to be
come substan

tially whole.

A black (2)

a) cat (no it isn'

t Friday the

13th) prowling
through these

pebbled bird-in
fested ground

b) s tastily expect

ant an especial

ly clawed–down
for breakfast'

s early morning
feast.

Are democracy' (5)

> *a) s basic freedom'*

s division-

of-powers be
ing tested

> *b) once again as in*

the USA of the

20s and 30s by
a nation desir

ous for getting-

> *c) things done via*

a strongish man
And are the Ger

man's need for
an orderly self-

> *d) assuming society*

antithetic to

British-like
stumbling

through imper

e) fectly compro

mised half-satis
fying design

s.

That once a *(2)*

a) gain early morn

ing swimmer a

ging in his de
sire for such

a cooling re

b) freshness a re

vitalizing
of limbs and

blood's sequen
tial soul-search

ings.

At the water' (2)

a) s edge the

early morn
ing waves flow

ing through
my time-reced

ing past as

b) if the lake

itself had
been personal

ly measur
ing my own re

ceptive imagin
ings.

White sea (2)

a) gulls surfac

ing the lake'

s wind-sourc
ed timeless

ly routed no-

b) wheres-else

but just-now
and those in

distinctive
callings dis

tantly away.

Sparrow (2)

a) s always and

everywhere

feeding on
those tasting

remnants of
left-over re

b) mains life-en

during no

questions
asked for e

ven timely-
sensed.

As so often (2)

a) in the animal

kingdom the

males just
used for breed

ing purpose
s but then do

b) mestically

released for a

lonely fort
une-free time-

telling.

The alway

s-present time
ly-doing jack-

of-all-trade
s and master

of-most Tommy
now almost in

visibly reclus
ive He's aging

now and look
ing that way.

Her head'

s become pin-
ball-small

as our alway
s-relevant

dean It's not
the size but

what's there
radiating

compact-phras
ings.

Something' *(2)*

a) s missing that

unquieting feel

ing of still
not realizing

what and where
at times so

b) strongly felt

as if an

arm or leg
not suffic

iently qualif
ying.

Brother and

sister swing
ing a together

ness of life'
s ups and

downs but may
be at their

small age in
tuned for more-

of-the-same.

Small bird (3)

a) s flying at

such a height

that their sha
dows fail to

b) reach ground-

base Some feel

that way at
their moment

s of greatest

c) success between

heaven and earth
shadowless

ly self–encom
passing.

If Columbus *(3)*

a) took seacows

for mermaids

it's not sur
prising that

b) he misplaced

America as

well Some per
sons I know all-

too-well have
difficulty

c) finding-out

what's right-

in-front of
their nose-

length.

Invisible (3)

a) *forces such as*

wind and love

help make this
world turn

b) *round on its*

impercepti

ble axis Why
then deny an

invisible God
creator even

c) *of the dark*

est ocean'

s depth and
the sky's blue–

sourced endless
spacefulness.

Tattooed (3)

a) bodies immediate

ly turn-me-off

not only be
cause of their

b) indwelling ugli

ness but also

because they re
mind me of

those Jewed
skinned-number

c) s collective

ly impregnat
ing death's

precisioned
route.

A cloudful (2)

a) *morning self-*

enclosing

as when the
curtains come

down on the
theatre's life-

b) *indwelling*

stage nothing

left except
that Shakespear

ean "the rest
is silence".

The lake

expressive
ly still smooth

ly sourced
to a recept

ively await
ing what's long

been said but
repetitively

now as ever–
before.

She kept (2)

a) asking herself

and her recept

ive mirror if
that smile

hers careful
ly prepared

b) could become

readily alive

to meet that
day's resource

ful time-be
ing.

Each unprepar

ed death of
friends and re

latives leave
s us with a

self-suspend
ing silence

as if prepar
ing for our

own phantomed-
decease.

Have these

timely chosen–
felt words be

come his most
reliable source

for a tension
ed-inhabit

ing momentary-
release.

Often what' (2)

a) s most person

ally sensed

reveals as
well those

self-inhabit
ing unspoken

b) silences

of the read

er's own
self-discover

ing raison
d'être. They felt
up to the occas
ion yet down

to its self-
exposing trans

parently-elus
ive intrica

cies.

Our one lone *(2)*

a) paddleboat

in the midst

of that self-
mirroring lake

skied well-bey
ond its even-

b) levelled sur

facing and

smoothly self-
reassuring

ly-felt con
templation

s.

Why isn't *(5)*

a) a common ling

uistic-histor

ical claim for a
sufficiently

b) sovereign

state of their

own Catalonian
self-reviving

plan whereas

c) the Kurds who

never possess
ed a state of

their own at
least five-divid

d) ed without a

common religion

language or e
ven an histori

cal past still

e) standing-up for

their own resol
utely fought-for

future Kurdistan.

For Warren *(2)*

a) a poem can

only display

an authentic
and genuine

ly curtained-i
dentity when

b) there's no-o

ther-way-left

than its inimi
cably individ

ually commend
ing-voice.

As 19th century

Italian poetry
lives and breath

es from its no-
longer-past

most especial
ly its incompar

ably cultural
importance.

He mostly *(3)*

a) feels-his-age

when an extreme

tiredness o
vercomes his

b) entire self-be

ing or while

bending-down
to reacquire

what's passed
so easily

c) through his

once deft left

fielder's most-
attending hand

s.

The more (3)

a) these poems

continue to

flow in and
out with these

b) time-receding

waves The more

too I feel the
ever slightly

heard Lord Jesus

c) walking most

assuredly on
those through-

calling waves-
of-His.

Small but in

tricately form
ed flowers

blossoming
from a stony

ground-base
as if to deny

an apparently
lifelessly

curtained-
future.

A pleasure (2)

a) boat soundless

ly appearing

at the other
Desenzano

side of the

b) lake as if

measuring
the intent of

my own distan
cing awareness

es.

Does a lang *(3)*

a) uage mirror

the basic quali

ties of a parti
cular people

b) as that abstract

German so con

ducive for philo
sophy music and

the natural

c) sciences or are

those especial
qualities them

selves language-
forming.

Can a once (4)

a) unifying Roman

Empire also be

come a model
for the future

b) of a linguist

ically religious

and historical
ly otherwise

ness of their

c) member-state

s A model it
most certainly

became for the
Spanish and Brit

c) ish empire

s yet equally

vulnerable
as the fall-of-

Rome itself.

Neither (4)

a) genes nor up

bringing can

fully explain
the why of my

b) (or other'

s) most indiv

idual–self
Did it become

leaned to its

c) own self-becom

ings or must

it as a valu
able ore be

d) cleansed of

time's most

self-forming
dross.

That tiny

lizard so slim
as it slither

s his way a
long the stone

wall's pre-estab
lishing time-

enduring cool
nesses.

As a child

I could never
have imagined

80-year-old
s the way we

are or at least
seem-to-be

almost young
er from day

to day's final
end-station.

These surround (2)

a) ing mountain

s have long

been voiced-in-
silence yet

their protect
ive eyes have

b) become wide-o

pen to the

wind's recurr
ing waved pre-

determining
shored-enclos

ures.

Catullus (2)

a) may have best

understood

these wave'
s time-invok

ing sadly re

b) sponsive

to his own
unfulfill

ing rhythmic
love-calling

s.

Is this lake

depthed in the
darkness of

its secretly
withholding

though ever-
present time

lessly recurr
ing-imagining

s.

If children *(4)*

a) first learn to

see feel and

think then
language it

b) self's but an

artificial

means of ex
pressing non-

lingual pre
existential

c) truths yet

first-class

poetry as
Shakespeare'

s penetrate
s linguistic

d) ally the depth

s of a personal

and persuasive
timelessly e

vident express
iveness.

2nd *Commandment* *(Moses) (3)*

a) Pleasure boat

s up and down

ing the tourist
ic length of

this self-enclos
ing lake Or is

b) it the delimit

ing mind and

senses of
these pleasure-

seeking tourist
s creating the

c) Lake of Garda

in the image

of their own
especial summer

ly expanding-
needs.

Soccer's *(2)*

a) the only com

petitive sport

I know where
the better

team often

b) fails of its

most esteem
ed lesser goal–

insisting vict
ory claim

s.

Watching *(2)*

a) our grandchild

ren growing–up

in a world
so different

from our own

b) distinctly

lessens the im
pact of our

oft dated so–
called timely–

advice.

During the (3)

a) 2nd World War

parents whether

German or Jew
ish valued the

b) future life of

their children

more than their
own Today though

those future–seek

c) ing values seem

more present or
better put self

ishly orient
ed.

It's been *(2)*

a) *long enough*

that baby-blue

chair hanging
unoccupied

from a bird-
infested tree

b) *waiting may be*

come the time

or even the
aspiring length

of it's just
hanging-there.

They're

thieves no ex
cuse for that

they steal e
ven from their

own brother
s and sister

s They're so
cute that Ger

man mothers
nick-name

their children
for those sneak

y birds affect
ionately refer

red to as spar
rows.

If it's true (4)

a) that mice bit

through the

cables of the
invading German

b) army thereby

halting their

advance once-
and-for-all

with the addit

c) ional help of

the frigid cold
then we should

lionize them
(the mice)

d) the secret wea

pon of the

Russian defen
se.

These light *(3)*

a) ly phrased

summerly Ital

ianate cloud
s have vanish

b) ed leaving be

hind but a

consummate
heavenly blue

almost the way

c) unwarranted

fears dissolve
into a most

promising daily-
perspective.

A tiredness

so intently
consuming per

haps even clos
er than he

realized to
death's signi

fying presen
ce.

Identity Cause (3)

a) Madeline com

plained her

mother alway
s needed a

b) cause to at

tain her self–

procuring end
implying that

Madeline her

c) self needed

nothing more
than what she

was and had
always-been.

When rhythm (5)

a) ic imbalance

hinders the

usual route
of a self-per

b) petuating

communicat

ion it's bett
er to slow-

down to a comm

c) only dialogued

more than
word–like ex

pressive
ness Some poem

d) s may years

later be asking–

me–back "Did
you really write

that Should I

e) answer" yes

but perhaps
from that self–

revealing other–
side–of–self.

When Turks *(3)*

a) and Jews no

longer feel

safe in Merkel'
s open-border

b) ed tolerant

and deeply hu

mane post-Ausch
witz Germany

something must

c) have gone wrong

but few realise
the whereabout

s of man's "o
therwise" nature.

Those addict (2)

a) ed to cheap

sex and blood

novels cheap
en their own

potential
ly otherwise

b) sensibility

And I'm most

certain they
also cheapen

that used–paper
as well.

Reading the

cloud's most un
certain route

awares us to
the timeless

ness of their
indwelling

persuasive-
silence

s.

Does one (4)

      a) write to im

      press one's

      mark on other
      s to open–

      b) out their own

      secretly pro

      tective inter
      ior claims or

      as an existen

      c) tial answer

      against death'
      s timeless

      hold or do we
      write simply be

      d) cause it's be

      come an essent

      ial part of
      our very–

      being.

A mild day

softly awaken
ed as my Rose

marie pillowed
in dream-rever

ies of a no
better or o

ther time only-
now only-here.

I'm weather (2)

a) ing myself in

to this just-

rightly-sens
ed pre-deter

mining day
until I've be

b) come envelop

ed in its own

most exclusive
ly voiced yet

transition
al-presence.

What we call *(4)*

a) and consider

as natural

isn't necess
arily bood

b) Nature may

have pre-es

tablished its
own rules but

The Good Lord'

c) s timelessly

securing word
s may reach

us to a high
er level of

d) His continual

ly creative

urging
s.

Are some (5)

> *a) "chance" meet*
>
> ings not real
>
> ly chanced at
> all We rare
>
> ly realise
> the effects
>
>
> *b) such meeting*
>
> s may have on
>
> others and also
> on our own
>
> continually
> dialogued–
>
>
> *c) person It's always*
>
> s best to measure
>
> one's words (as
> good poets should
>
> do) to the per
> son and circum

d) stance that

they (the word

s) may inhabit
even beyond

their perhaps
limited intent –

I've always

e) questioned those

wisdom–moralis
ing–words of

some poets (Goethe
included) but now

I've begun doing
much–the–same.

A first walk

on our seclud
ed boardwalk

shading protect
ively new born

birds and per
haps conducive

as well for se
cluded new–

born poem
s.

Catch-me-if

you can a children'

s game breath
lessly pursu

ing phantomed
shadowing

s of an elus
ive no-where

s-mine.

High noon

of these open-
aired Italian

ate mid-sum
mered days the

eternal blue
of such time

lessly self-
invoking contem

plation
s.

That repetit

ive jungle
drum-beat

self-insist
ent recall

ing our primit
ive darkly in

habiting
lower-levell

ed instinct
s.

That question (5)

a) able line bet

ween poetry

and prose
Is it the tone

b) that predeter

mines the in

tent as well
the image or

its absence

c) the mood-inhab

iting or the
pedagogic

teacher's/min
ister's intent

d) It may at

times remain

possible to
bring both-to

gether yet

e) often at the

cost of a unify
ing raison d'

être.

Those who (2)

a) at a distant

glance can i

dentify real
from bleached

or wigged blond-
pretension

b) s may also be

those who real

ise the multi-sen
sual qualit

ies of really
good modern

poetry.

The German (2)

a) s of Hitler'

s times may

have looked
much-the-same

as today but

b) appearance

seldom symp
toms our more

than skin-deep
apparent-

self.

Philemon *(3)*

a) and Baucis

may have pre

dated our own
aging year

b) s But we do

hope The Good

Lord will say
"I'll give

them another

c) decade or so

to exemplify

the true merit
s of marriage'

s sacred cause."

Lying back

in our easy
chairs with the

lake's accust
omed closeness

we leisure these
late afternoon

hours as if
time's become

ours-for-the
asking.

This early

morning lake
calmed to a

wave-certify
ing mosaic

of wind-ex
panding self-

satisfying ex
pressive

ness.

After re-read (4)

a) *ing Dover Beach*

by way of Samuel

Barber I too
began listen

b) *ing intently*

for the wave'

s perhaps Soph
oclean message

If life's a

c) *continuing*

dialogue why
haven't these

waves revealed
their indeciph

d) *erable but al*

ways incessant

ly demanding
message.

The poet' (2)

a) s mood-mind

wandering

as Wordsworth'
s clouds sha

dowing those
touched sensed

b) seen until

once again

home-based
in the word'

s most confident
ial expressive

ness.

Some of (3)

a) *these women*

here seem as

if dressed-up
for an out-com

b) *ing fashion-*

parade walking

gracefully
down the pebb

led aisle of
this modest

c) *hotel with*

such a color

fully flour
ishing pre-de

signed self-
importance.

Some of (4)

a) these possible

still–life

s hardly re
main still

b) for long that

stone–contem

plating liz
ard or those

busy bird–

c) lengthed sha

dowings life
ful all yet

with little
time or in

d) clination

for purposing

after–thought
s.

That pop (2)

a) singer "found

his voice"

though it
sounded like

most all the

b) others guitar-

based even
those baby-face

cutely insinuate
ing love-call

s.

It's perhap (4)

a) *s not-by chance*

that Catullus'

Sirmione has
become my own

b) *Both of us*

poetically

aristocrat
ic by nature

Both of our
life pre-deter

c) *mined by a wo*

man his to a

life-long Cir
cean servitude

of his over
wrought passion

d) *s whereas mine*

more guided in

the calm stream
s of a life-en

chanting love-
spell.

Sparrow (3)

a) s always inno

cently appear

ing that short
hop-sized-and-

b) jump tastied

hungry look

only satisfied
when it final

ly flies off

c) leaving behind

not even a
remote trace of

somewhere
s-else.

Globalised

persons as that
paella waiter

in Garda grand
parented from

four decidedly
other national

ities so varied
his personal i

dentifying
crisis.

Her teeshirt

proclaiming
"life is a

beach" But
what for ex

ample of that
deadly perhap

s life-ensur
ing Omaha Beach.

Even the (2)

a) Donald Trump

s learn in

time that mak
ing enemies

out of friend

b) s remain much

easier than
making friend

s out of for
mer enemie

s.

They don't (5)

a) realise it but

they should

Europe's time
is over after

b) twice saving

them from them

selves those 2
hideous self-

destructive
wars Europe'

s time is o
ver even its

c) great cultural

epochs let's

close the book
on them and

try to dis

d) tinguish the

others most
likely to be

come burdened
with the same

e) mistakes or

perhaps of more

creatively o
ther one

s.

He couldn' *(3)*

a) t face-up to

his own other

wise mirror
ing image it

b) kept talking

back denying

the similar
ity until he

took that mir

c) ror down and

began living
in a mirror

less world
of his own.

Blood relat *(4)*

a) ions may slow

ly become di

luted or e
ven from the

b) beginning

discover path

s to self-be
coming Blood-o

riented famil

c) ies usually re

claim themselve
s in a clan–

oriented soc
iety when the

d) I rarely speak

s its own self-

determining
ways.

There' (2)

a) s a closeness

in the air

expressive
ly nearing to

what's tight

b) ly exposed

drawing-in
immersing an

indwelling pre
sent-perspect

ive.

Words have an *(2)*

a) inborn right to

declare the

possible ex
tension of their

inherent pre-giv
en domain But

b) if not used

or overly in

tended lose in
time their self-

substantial
raison d'être.

A quiet rain

sensitizing
the skin's

touched-through
reflection

s opening-out
a view far

beyond the eye'
s accommodating

distancing
s.

A black bird'

s shadowing i
mage on those

newly painted
yellow wall

s leaving be
hind but an

indwelling fear
of still unre

solving tens
ions.

A love-marr (2)

a) iage should

never be allow

ed to lose its
sensual embra

cing preferen
ces Otherwise

b) it will deter

iorate in to

a cool distan
cing from its

once so intend
ed promising

s.

All these *(3)*

a) white-sailing

doves and those

boats languish
ing a wind–

b) still vacancy

white too if

only purposed
to counter the

darkening

c) threat of the

lake's invisib
ly depthed–se

clusion
s.

Can one

really write-
off what con

tinues to
plague those

darkly sensed
phases of

night's irre
trievable

warning
s.

Are Gatsby' *(3)*

a) s bookless

book-cover

s only a de
ceptive mean

b) s of acquir

ing an educat

ed air of
cultural

know-how
but question

c) ing as Nath

aniel West the

artificial
ity of timely

initial impress
ions.

Precision (2)

a) *as with Rilke'*

s Thing Poems

or Kafka'
s surrealist

ic short stor
ies remains the

b) *best possible*

means of mirror

ing what's
most elusive

ly uncertain
ed.

Good reader (6)

a) s today are

few and far

between as the
poet they must

b) allow the poem

to speak for

itself without
pre-conviction

s or ideological

c) value-judgment

s They should

reread each
poem several

times even o

d) rally to deci

pher subtletie
s of linguist

ic usage They
should remain o

e) pen to other

wise ways of ex

pressive mean
ings Sometime

s I feel the

f) reader may have

a more difficult
task than the

poet himself.

Garcilaso' (4)

a) *s such perfect*

ly fit sonnet

s of a purity
even beyond

b) *their own ling*

uistic length

may not stay
will with the

Catholic churches'
believe in origin

c) *al sin or parod*

ies of Cervantes'

oft wickedly-
sourced pen but

beauty maint
ains its own

d) *staying-right*

s for this pre–
Mozartean

scribe dead
at 33.

These recurr *(2)*

a) ing winds seem

to have arrived

just–in–time
for my morn

ing's wake–up
poems invisib

b) ly listened

to the sound

less rhythms
of their self–

reflective
voice.

Is color

its own self–
creating mast

er silent e
merging as

the Greek's
gods and god

esses celebrat
ing life's im

pulsing renew
als.

Renaming (3)

a) streets for a

more our-time-

amenable-mast
er satisfy

b) ing the pre

sent all-encom

passing need
for political

correctness
while that same

c) street seems un

changed from

its daily suffi
cient prefer

able route-
timing.

Whatever (4)

a) may divide

nations and e

ven persons in
these irrever

b) ently question

able times–of–

ours still Most-
all would agree

that love's

c) the true pre-

determining
force that keep

s our planet
still revolving

d) around its

light–suffi

cient way
s.

For George *(3)*

a) If the bird

s hadn't been

previously
created would

b) we ever have

thought of fly

ing ourselve
s' creativity

constantly
in need of

c) pre-designed

suddenly rele

vant for our
own next–step

forwards.

She became (4)

a) *so personal*

ly involved

in that paper
back novel

b) *that it had*

become quite

questionable
(at least for

me) whether she'
s ever find

c) *her way out*

as those teen

agers in Thai
land lost in

the darkness
of a primeval

c) *cave enclosing*

even the sha

dows of their
ever-lessen

ing person.

With such a (4)

a) profusion of

checks and bal

ances it seem
s that the

b) so-called demo

cratic process

will find it
increasing

ly difficult

c) to ever reach

decisive conclu
sions more like

one of those
artificial

d) ly sourced

Thomas Mann'

s long-rout
ed sentence

s.

Fake news (6)

a) is not only

directly lying

in the Goebbel
s tradition

b) of its main

tained long and

loud enough
it will in time

make itself

c) fully believed

or the biblical
Satanic way of

half and quarter
truths or report

d) ing only one

side to an at

least 2-sided
happening

or insinuat

e) ing what's not

factually so
We're all more

or less vict
ims of wish

f) ful-thinking

that heart

and soul of
fake news.

Italian (3)

a) ate late after

noon summer

shadowing
s less weight

b) ed more soft

ly express

ive than those
autumnal one

s brooding
fear and in

c) some birds

the inherent

tensions of
their most

necessary on
coming flight.

Each time *(2)*

a) I'm called-to-

write a new

beginning
as if I'd

never written
anything else

b) before It's

like the touch

ing closeness
of Rosemarie'

s light–surr
ounding smile.

When I read *(3)*

a) too much and

all-at-once

of a really
first-rate

b) poet as Garcil

aso overwhelm

ing my own
poetic self

with an imitat

c) ive style too

derivative
to become per

sonally sour
ced as my-own.

To measure (4)

a) *presents by*

their store-dis

covering price-
tag reveals

b) *more-than-e*

nough of mer

cenary value-
judgment

s That's pretty-

c) *much-the-same*

as their sport
ing Olympic

medals achiev
ed by other

d) *s yet now*

prestigious

ly up-for-sale
at a local

pawn-shop.

After a teacher- *(4)*

a) student concert

Musical virtuos

ity may be an
audience-plea

b) ser but it dis

plays most often

a limited sense
of a truly depth

ed-musicality

c) A lot depends

on the choice
of composer

s Better by far
(for violinists)

d) Corelli Bach

Mozart and Beet

hoven than their
Paganini and Fritz

Kreisler!

For a marri *(4)*

a) ageable woman it

may become

difficult to
judge her suit

b) or's true in

tention

s mainly be
cause women (how

ever sensitive
ly attuned) sense

c) such thing

s quite differ

ently from a
manly approach

but also be
cause the suitor

d) may not have

realized his

own unbecoming
purposing

s.

Mallarmé

may have poet
ically discov

ered the aesthet
ic useful

ness of women'
s oriental fan

s creating a
wind of color

ful expectat
ions.

Waiting for (2)

a) just the right

word somehow re

minds me of
those patient

ly endowed fish

b) ermen also wait

ing for the un
likely pull of

a fish's death-
intending appet

ite.

After Victor Frankl (2)

a) Don't rub-it-

in that mis

take or guilt
may become an

indigenous
part of his or

her very-being

b) Most mistakes

are first re
vealed by the

guilty-one –
Set an example

be kind and for
give.

Cypresses

conforming
this lake-

side with at
least their

own self-per
petuating

upstanding uni
formity.

Little girl (3)

a) s may still

highly approve

of imitating
their mother

b) s facial ex

pression

s but when
they're not so

little anymore

c) they begin to

route their
newly self-dis

covering facial-
identity-cause.

Often it (2)

a) seems that only

with the snow

owl's special
approval does

the fully appar

b) ent harvest moon

take-on its
secretly enlight

ened time-flour
ishing

s.

An English- *(2)*

a) appropriate

Sunday hat

with all the
necessary

ribbons and a
visor shadow

b) ing the most

intimately

possible relig
ious–contem

plation
s.

Are these (3)

a) *time-extend*

ing waves se

cretly sourc
ed from the

b) *wind's persist*

ent question

ings as these
ever–present

poems demand

c) *ing their own*

rights through
my most necess

ary craftsman'
s resolve.

"Not a soul

in sight" as if
souls could be

come astutely
present or

that eye could
reestablish

their invisib
ly sensed-ap

pearance.

When it's (4)

a) become tradition

al for even

those robust
English gentle

b) men to rise

to the call of

Handel's famed
Hallelujah

Messiah's

c) chorus still

perhaps faint
ly mirroring

a Christian
thankfulness

d) for the sub

lime words and

deeds of Christ
our heavenly

savior.

Dialogue (3)

a) s especially

political one

s should never
begin with an

b) implicitly

high-handed

morally super
ior "I told

you so" atti

c) tude but posit

ively in search
of commonly shar

ed-interest
s.

Our balcony' (2)

a) s high-level

view of the

lake's spacious
ly expansive

wave–calling

b) s leaves me

more wondering
about its under

water invisible
life's darkly

inhabiting.

Birds here (2)

a) of whatever

size or color

seems as New
York business

men most al
ways in-a–

b) hurry for what

and where re

maining for us
continual

ly unanswer
able question

ings.

"Anchors (2)

a) away" the navy'

s call from

all that had
anchored its

sailors to
their earth–

b) bound claim

s now opening–

out the ocean'
s deadly time-a

waiting uncer
taintie

s.

Three of (2)

a) Spain's great

mystical poet

s of Jewish
descent and yet

they lacked the

b) "blood purity"

to justify their
ardently espous

ed Catholic
calling

s.

"2ⁿᵈ Guessing"

often more
like extend

ing one's
own way of

seeing and do
ing things in

to the other
s rightly self-

establishing
domain.

Aunt Nicki (3)

a) *"the only one*

who understood

me as an adol
escent" (my eld

b) *est sister Doris)*

wasn't capable

of bringing-up
her own child

ren Full of the
youngest child'

c) *s spoiled ego*

ism and yet

also of an o
penly loving–

empathy.

For many Ger (4)

a) mans discover

ing what their

parents or grand
parents had

b) done during

those fateful 12

years could be
come a life-

long trauma But

c) for Heinrich

Himmler's
much-loved

daughter she re
mained a life-

d) long ardent admir

er of his per

son and life-
long "heroic"

deed
s.

My mother *(4)*

a) saw the small

things in life

as a jewelled
ring on the

b) streets or that

extra penny

for a chocolate
soda and made

them feel big

c) whereas my fa

ther realized
what he thought

as the big thing
s in life and

d) pocketed them

for his most

substantial
gain.

There's noth *(2)*

a) ing so import

ant for a child

as a parental lov
ing-care which

I enjoyed to
the fullest

b) except perhap

s the opposite

that may help
cause a tru

ly independ
ent spirit as

Rosemarie.

One of those

thought-possibili
ties left him

self-balancing
an impression

ed-intent.

Before the

storm came
we shut every

thing down
that we became

closed in a
soundless dark

ness and slept
in irretriev

able dream-span
s.

When Europe (2)

a) with its long

and varied hist

ory of anti-semit
ism has now tak

en the moral

b) upper-hand in

unduly critic
ising Israel'

s last hope of
Jewish-surviv

al.

Even the 4th (2)

    a) of July's fire

    works seem as

    but a pale i
    mitation of

    how the heaven
    s lit-up last

    b) night's no-where

    s-to-be-seen

    except light
    ning's vividly

    awakened heaven
    ly appealing

    s.

What an unassum (3)

a) *ing delight watch*

ing Rosemarie'
s child–like
curious eye

b) *s innocently*

taking-the-mea

sure of person
s she'd so tem

porarily sour

c) *ced for perhap*

s the very
first evasive

momentary
time-hold.

We know what' (4)

a) s better-for-

you a condescend

ing almost paren
tal attitude

b) to a people

that's lived

through hundred
s of years of

persecution
also quite often

c) at the hand

s of its new

ly unselected
advisers I smell

a rat those
underground anti–

d) semitic Jews

gnawing at the

very basis of
their own people'

s most necessary
survival-link.

Is a guilty *(2)*

a) conscience The

Good Lord's

way of remind
ing us of his

eternally a
biding command

b) ments and/or

the other-side-

of-self accus
ing its mirror

ed image of
double-dealing

s.

Some women (2)

a) *are just-too-*

pretty to be

looked away
from My Rose

marie in her 80s

b) *still tops that*

unappointed
list of select

ive facial–feat
uring

s.

After the *(3)*

a) storm a time-

appropriat

ing silence
almost innocent

b) ly reclaiming

a once–as–it–

had–been Even
the SS return

ed to their
families life

c) went on despite

the millions of

dead as it al
ways was in

its usual daily–
spent routine.

Call it poet *(2)*

a) ic-prose or a

time–reclaim

ing thought–
poetry that

must–be–said

b) whatever you

name it in
its best–possi

ble way of
dressing–it

self–up.

Early morn

ing swimmers
feeling–out

that lengthen
ing reach of

their body's
newly rhythmic

ally attuned
self–becom

ing.

"I agree" (3)

a) may be comfort

ing for the

poetic husband'
s recreating

b) familiarity

But he never

theless would
prefer "I've

never seen or

c) sensed it that

way" of a poet'
s delving in to

unexplored terri
tory.

Short-cut *(4)*

a) s were my child-

like way of ad

venturing out-
of-bounds

b) through some

one's (most

ly A. B.'s)
front-walk

or back yard

c) on-the-way

to grade school
But short-cut

s have contin
ued in my own

d) poetic way

of front or

back discover
ies of a lin

guistic other
wiseness.

Such familiar (2)

a) ground here Hotel

Astoria on-and-

off for decade
s and yet al

most totally un

b) familiar face

s which have
also become

that pre-deter
mining land

scaping.

Both Beethoven (3)

a) and Brahms re

flectively walked with

their hands clasp
ed tightly be

b) hind their back

s Was it simply

an unconscious
Brahmsian imitat

ion or do
such rhythmic

c) resources indi

cate something

about that
through-sound

ing musical–
intent.

If each sea *(3)*

a) son perpetuate

s its own pre

determining
say and we'

b) ve become en

compassed by

each and e
very as the

weather-vane

c) turning which

ever direct
ion the wind

will be decid
ing.

Are river (4)

a) s immersed

in a change
able history

at times

b) quietly even

silently flow
ing their

self-chosen
way at other

c) s rapidly

bare-faced

stone-intense
Or are they

simply witness

d) es of an un

told history
timelessly

self-absorb
ing.

Early morning (5)

a) dove's repeated

love-call

s as if the
night's dark

b) ness hadn't

been sufficient

ly explored
for their touch

ed-through

c) together long

ingness and
these irrecon

cilable wind
s fleeing from

d) an unknown myster

ious source

Daphne-like
as if she hadn'

t already been

e) timelessly

treed to es
cape her ardent

ly pursuing
lover.

To the North (2)

a) these time-allur

ing mountain

s so evident
ly clear even

more so than
their unerring

b) intent as Mac

beth's Burnham

Woods drawing
constantly near

er to their
time–fulfilling

conclusion.

If as they *(4)*

a) maintain the

violin viola

and cello had
been sourced

b) here Why didn'

t Corelli and

Haydn the great
instrumental

innovator

c) s traverse

this sound–
purifying lake

to truly in
habit their

d) own chastely-

classical unify

ing–intention
s.

It's only (4)

   a) when the varied

   colors of these

   Italianate
   flowers began

   b) growing-on-me

   as if I too

   had become sun–
   brightened

   and water

   c) ing through

   their time–ex
   posures that

   as The Great
   Bard realized

   d) the penetrat

   ing intent of

   "the mind's
   eye".

At coffee- (2)

a) time in Lazise

a young lady

appeared so
totally over-

flowing bosom
ed that she

b) seemed to have

become a liv

ing replica of
those ancient

fertility god
esses.

Nervous (2)

a) laughter (there

s plenty of

that here)
at times so

uneases my
scratching

b) the left (less

concealing)

arm for a
sufficient

ly adequate
response.

Christian (2)

a) themes so god

ly sourced be

come just as
stale as any

other if re

b) peatedly con

signed to
those same

familiar
routes of cli

chéd permanen
cy.

I won't (3)

a) be tested by

fire or water or

even every o
ther way except

b) my own repeat

ed flesh and

blood arousing
to their half-

nakedly expos

c) ing-claims on

my seeming
ly defense

less imagin
ings.

It's hard to *(3)*

a) measure the

length and depth

of words (only
time will tell)

b) because some

are quite cap

able as the
blow fish of ex

panding or e

c) ven contract

ing their own
less diminish

ing expressive
ness.

Why that (3)

a) most general

fear of silence

and readied
need for noise

b) perhaps because

silence mean

s aloneness
that makes one

feel and ap

c) pear unwanted

unloved out
side that group

sense-of-
belonging.

Right out of (2)

a) *Africa those*

primeval self-

perpetuat
ing drum-beat

s awakening

b) *those most*

darkly-primit
ive sensual

ground-based
urging

s.

These momen (5)

a) *tary changeable*

clouds a heaven

ly mosaic beauty
fying the Ital

b) *ianate summer*

sky with The

Creator's sheer
unlimited creat

ive resource

c) s reminding

of a lesser
lower-level map

ping-out one
s own creative

d) designs that

four-sided

street map'
s homebred

until the out

e) er reach of

high school'
s anonymous

poetic start-
ups.

Sometime (2)

a) s these poem

s seem to

take-in-account
the particular

always change
able person

b) remaining close-

to and even

captivated by
this unreliev

ing poetic
time-spell.

Mixed-signal *(3)*

a) s or call it

cross–purposing

s that at time
s he dreamt him

b) self alone in

a sail boat in

the midst of
the lake's

serene quiet
udes but still

c) so dependent

on the wind'

s taken this
Thursday's

day–off.

How much has (5)

    a) The American be

come a daily

part of my i
dentity-cause

    b) 1944 sailor-

clothed for that

patriotic song
of an unsung

hero in the Solo

    c) mons a partial

smash-up while
avidly intent on

a Notre Dame foot
ball game a

d) logical choice

for a Jewish–

Protestant
sport's lover

or as Rosemarie
finds it my

e) still perpetu

ating Monday
taste for a

duly-courted ham
burger.

A big man *(3)*

a) with a very

little dog on

the leash mak
ing him feel

b) even bigger

than that very

little dog feel
s even more

that little

c) ness leading

him to lesser
scented find-a

bout
s.

Sculptured

mountain
s modelled to

a pre-histor
ic abstract

unidentifi
able creative

ly anonymous
source.

The card *(5)*

a) s had perhap

s become his

most confiden
tial partner

b) for others it

could-have-

been the more
dangerous

alcohol He
played complete

c) ly alone a

young clean-

cut-looking
man with the

card's faces

d) turned up as

if they could
have become wo

men in their
steadied glance

couldn't conceal

e) his aloneli

ness on a bright
most inviting

Italianate
Monday after

noon.

Small talk (4)

a) smalls-down the

person who spec

ialises in say
ing just the

b) appropriate

things at just

the right time
that no one

feels uncom
fortable and no

c) one needs to

think much a

bout what isn'
t thinkable

at all as
if time had

d) become such

an expend

able daily
self–attuning

item.

Here and (2)

a) now it's be

come wind the

more-so per
sistently

claiming

b) these wave'

s surfacing
intent contin

ually assur
ing a no-ways-

back.

Looking twice *(5)*

a) to realise why

that word didn'

t seem self–
situated mis

b) spelled be

cause neglect

ed so long
that it couldn'

t phrase itself

c) back to what

would propose
an opened dict

ionary Simply
said some per

d) sons too seem out-

of–place must

become second–
thoughted in

to reserved and

e) fully comfort

chairs with match
ing subdued color

ing place-mat
s as well.

The lake *(2)*

a) daily adrift

with wind-

spells chang
ing direction

s either here

b) or there yet

a continuity
of redefining

its most un
certain identi

ty-cause.

Thieve (3)

a) s those early-

to-bed early-

to-rise sparr
ows dipping

b) suddenly low

to retrieve

those not-to-
be-forgotten

morsels of

c) what had be

come the left-
overs from a

sunset love-
enthralled e

vening meal.

Broken

clouds (or at
least they

seemed that
way) spacious

ly attending
to the heaven'

s alternate
blue-envelop

ing design
s.

Some women (3)

a) *may enjoy re*

vealing their

softly sensed
bodily warmth

where other

b) *s prefer their*

tastefully
chosen dress–

designs but
both fully a

ware of those

c) *curious and*

admiring men'

s eyes complet
ing that fully

formed woman
ly-presence.

Two direct (2)

a) ioned the lake'

s spreading-
out the un

told depth of
its darkly-sens

ed omnipresen

b) ce whereas we'

re left with
only those sur

facing timely-
kept wind-

waved dependen
ces.

Bringing the (2)

a) bible up-to-

date with "the

spirit-of-the
times" its peren

nial mentor
not only denie

b) s The Good Lord'

s omnipotence

but the univer
sality of His

word's time
less relevan

ce.

High School (2)

a) and college

left little

mark on my
most present

sensibility
but their re

b) flective lone

liness suffic

ed to help
record those

momentary
time-lapse

s.

An all-alone (4)

a) lady as if

hatted from a

previous cen
tury came yes

b) with her equal

ly catching–

up out–dated
husband down

the aisle to

c) our Astoria

beach that
Rosemarie and

I began to
feel once a

d) gain as perfect

ly situated

youngster
s.

If when we' (3)

a) re aging we

might forget

the names of
persons close-

to-us it

b) might also

mean that
name never real

ly depthed an
understand

ing of that

c) person for us

Names that remain
essentially relev

ant if not
they're easily

forgotten.

The half of (3)

a) a rainbow as if

to say its mean

ing now only
half-relevant

b) as those half-

completed poem

s that stopped
as Schubert'

s Unfinished
Symphony before

c) their otherwise

signifying pre

sence had be
come active

ly essential.

Absented- *(4)*

a) minded as my

father pre-

occupied with
what may seem

b) necessary

and as–for–

me those poem
s waiting to

be dressed in
what's signifi

c) cantly self-ex

posing Perhaps

they should
have become

collectively
called "Bikini

d) poems" self-re

vealing but

only half–de
sirously

so.

Chekhovian *(2)*

a) open-ending

s could also

become a back–
room escape–

route as my
mother's Vien

b) nese Jewish

friend out the

back door while
the Gestapo

just coming–
in the front

one.

If "Good marr

iages are made
in heaven" where

did those o
ther-ones de

rive their
self–destruct

ive disabling
power

s.

Can a nation

as Poland di
vided so long

develop an
indigenous

culture or
are Chopin and

Weinberg also
inhabiting

a cultural di
vide.

Snails housed (2)

a) in a permanent

stillness
as slowly kept

as their drawn–
down phrasing

b) s though tast

ed with the

varied pleasure
s of this sum

mer's sumptuous
greenness.

These apple *(3)*

a) s still hard

but ripening

in to a pre
determining

b) fullness And

I with aging

eyes and sen
ses but ripen

ing too to

c) that suddenly

unexpected
fall once a

gain ground-
based.

Who would (3)

a) want to spend

an evening

with their
grandparent

s Nothing quite

b) so uninterest

ing when you'
re 17 or 18

Were we any
different we

may think we

c) deserve a better

chance but we
really don'

t It's another
world both-way

s-round.

I'm becoming *(3)*

a) more of paper

myself not

only my book
worm eldest

sister She

b) chose those

genuinely
worth re-tim

ing as Jane
Austen and

Henry James

c) whereas I pap

er the future
with my own

lesser-lived
expectation

s.

I have-it- *(3)*

a) all or better

said it in

habits me
love faith

b) and the dis

tant hope for

an indwelling
sanctity better

sourced than
my daily misgiv

c) ing Why then

as Wallace Stev

ens' desiring
"more more

more".

If we know (3)

a) ourself best

(though blem

ished by a dis
figuring

b) self-certain

ty) that's the

best way to
realise the

difference

c) to other's

most conceal
ing self–sub

jective appear
ance

s.

If one's on- *(2)*

a) the-wrong-track

(as so many to

day) Is it still
possible to

change train

b) s redirect

ing oneself to
a pre-determin

ing if still
obscurely un

certain fut
ure.

Why are (2)

a) those so-good

in chess dis

covering the
necessitie

s of 4 or e
ven 5 moves ad

b) vanced their

own life's

bloodlessly
artificial

time–reclaim
ing mistaken–

identity.

It's not a (2)

a) *question of one*

poem more or

less then each
remains as a

momentary

b) *world unique*

ly fashioned
to a self-ex

pressive unify
ing and self-

revealing i
dentity-cause.

On Hanni's

photograph
s There's an

elusive feel
ing to what

can't quite
be resolved

but neverthe
less haunting

ly otherwise.

Why match

yourself a
gainst other

poets "to
each his own"

a singular
choice of no

wheres and no-
one's else

s.

Church bell

s in a medieval
South Tyrolean

town continual
ly self-intun

ed yet some
how now lack

ing a self-dis
tinguishing

personal-re
sponse.

He's on his (2)

> *a) high horse*
>
> once again
>
> teaching who
> ever will or
>
> won't attend

> *b) to his self-*
>
> resounding
> most self-as
>
> sured newspap
> er-conviction
>
> s.

Certain *(3)*

a) things will re

main intimate

ly English
afternoon tea

beef and kidney

b) pie that clipp

ed-off accent
ed-English

cultivated
lawns and the

until recent

c) ly self-perpet

uating quality
of its own in

sular literary
tradition.

Brixen *(4)*

a) (Bressanone)

cloisters the

word-inspired
Jewish prophet

b) s neverthe

less stigmat

ised with that
pointed hat

pointedly

c) displaying

their outcast
post-Jesuan ex

istence Why
then wasn't

d) the Jew-Jesus

signified in

that self-de
meaning way.

These rising

Tyrolean hill
s carry-me-up

beyond the
vast reaches

of my own
celebrating

poetic-climb
s.

Young women (2)

a) here display

ing their half-

naked suggest
ive claim

s as the Baal

b) prostitut

ing Israel to
its ground-

base fruitful-
desiring

s.

These still

wooded Tyrol
ean hills as

piring claim
s well beyond

reach of their
cloud-ingather

ing timeless
perspective

s.

This morn

ing moon as a
pre-exposing

sage slowly fa
ding in to

its express
ively sensed–

forgetful
ness.

Sirmione a

gain as famil
iar as that

new round of
unfamiliar

faces testing–
out a tourist'

s hotel's ex
pendable

gracious
ness.

The reach

of this untouch
able sky seem

s even beyond
the length

and depth of
human contemplat

ion.

Raphael our

retarded son
now 55 seems

capable of
mastering e

very form known
and unknown of

phobically
intensed–sensi

bilitie
s.

Jaccottet (6)

a) leaves shadow

s grow in to

their own ex
panding size

and self-quest

b) ioning length

until they've
certained their

own child-like
sense of timed–

c) expressive

ness It's not

the said but
the undertone

that leaves im

d) pressions as

voiceless child-
like intonat

ions Time cruel
s such scarce

e) ly remember

ed intention

s while he's
retaining them

somehow and

f) neverthe

less as his
own special

ly his.

I imagine *(4)*

a) if clouds

could speak it

would most cer
tainly in a sub

b) tly impression

istic French

Constable might
disagree here

but clouds lang

c) uage a transient

sense of an in
volving still

ness purpos
ing an almost

d) intangible

rang of color–

like intonat
ions.

Not even

this insatiable
heat can blunt

my need for
an impress

ive coolness
of phrased-

sensing
s.

One death- *(2)*

a) articulat

ing slap and

that unawared
stinging in

sect blood-ex
posed no exten

b) uating fear

of a timed-

suffering but
just a momen

tary no-long
er-now.

Vague though (2)

a) *neverthe*

less amiable

mood-shifting
impression

s of a late
afternoon

b) *breeze restor*

ing time's

most necessary
self-certify

ing shadow
ings.

Time-sequen

ces as with
Jaccottet may

childhood us
again impress

ioned in a
still unrequit

ed most person
al response.

As they (3)

a) say "time

will take its

course" But what
if the wrong

b) kind of people

d the helm

And what if
it's like that

plague boat
1349 with only

c) rats steering

their intruded way
though time

will neverthe
less take-its-

own-course.

After that

night–storm
only the light

early morning
rains soften

ing that previous
once pervasive

ly awared–im
pact.

Children'

s once imagin
ing fears not

completely
healed remain

oft only for
dream's self–es

tablishing
repetitive

time–reclaim
ings.

Hotel Astoria *(Sirmione) (2)*

a) If age and

experience

really matter
we've become

the historical
heirs to a

b) hotel through

our time-atten
ding more than

a half-century
if irregular

yearly-return
s.

How to counsel (2)

a) an aging friend

and fellow Christ

ian caught in
that Circe-

Catullus trap
of beautiful

b) women's enti

cing spell o

ver their once
timely suffi

cient marital-
vows.

If you listen (2)

a) hard-enough

(listening

to the rain'
s unevenly re

petitive call

b) ings) it may

be waiting for
your own still

uncertained
if only tenta

tively assured–
response.

Kafka person (2)

a) al of Kafka

original

most always
s on the out

side of no–
ways–in to

b) what may also

prove to be

coming an in
side–out of

an irrevocab
ly uncertain

thereness.

Familiar (3)

a) *place familiar*

time and yet

the perspect
ive's changed

b) *the heat's re*

ceded the after

noon 4:20 sha
dows once a

gain dominant
ly suspected

c) *of regaining*

a poised on

coming perhap
s even last

ing–initiat
ive.

Sometime *(4)*

a) s the intend

ed poem stray

s amiss be
cause I fail

b) to poetise

what may have

been intended
and/or be

cause the poem

c) insists what

it doesn't de
serve its say-

so and/or
because the in

d) tending idea

doesn't re

lease that es
pecial know-

how.

That stray

bird warmed
below the sur

face for his
most taste

able find a
poet in its

own right
though perhap

s to a more
satisfying

conclusion.

Have these (2)

a) morning wave

s washed a

way my dream
s and left

me vacantly

b) receive the

necessary

words on their
own but not so

constantly e
vident-term

s.

Georgie *(3)*

a) Porgie" always

s the first

to realise
his money-gain

b) s while taking

the stairs down

with his in
cipient market-

perspective
s reminded at

c) the very last

moment to court

the only real
love of his

time-pursuing
life-style.

The alway

s Italian
ate-blue of

the sky's irre
concilably

distancing
perspective

s.

That Lake *(3)*

a) of Garda pleas

ure boat so

early sound
lessly pursu

b) ing its chart

ered course

as if time
itself had be

come reconcil

c) ed to its

daily most
necessary

need
s.

A real poet (2)

a) as Jaccottet

begins at child

hood–time in
remembrance

of what con

b) tinues to per

sist as those
so oft unre

membered
dream

s.

At some prim *(2)*

a) eval time those

Desenzano

hills across
the lake had

been soften

b) ed-down to ex

pose their
newly acquired

timeless–per
spective

s.

It's not (5)

a) *always necess*

ary for a

depthed-read
er to reattune

his or her own

b) *perspective*

s to the poet'
s less famil

iar word-ex
pressive

ness where

c) *I most assured*

ly sit as a

pre-establish
ed-center-

piece the lake'

d) *s opening-*

out its com
plementary

vistas to my
most poetical

e) ly sensed here-

and–now and

most certain
ly nowhere

s–else.

When time

and place be
come an insepar

ably unifying
cause and the

unspoken speak
s even louder

than just-the-
right-word's

timelessly
concealing.

When a poem *(2)*

a) doesn't reveal

more than its

primary intent
ion as a land-

locked salmon

b) born without a

reconciling
need for spawn

ing in foreign
water

s.

That morning

moon again half-
sized slowly fa

ding in to in
visibly oft-

timed precept
ions.

Umbrella (2)

a) s of all

shapes color

s and size
s uplifting

their hesi

b) tantly aspir

ing thought
s to such

heavenly
transcend

ing height
s.

Borghetto

at dusk in
such a pro

tective medie
val town even

the house
s seem as if

suspending
an irreconcil

ably purposed
time-length.

The mind'

> s not enough
> to certain
>
> that depth-
> range of a
>
> poetically-
> awared instinct
>
> ual-express
> iveness.

These billow

> ed clouds hold
> ing softly
>
> to the dedi
> cated rite
>
> s of their
> heavenly-sour
>
> ced timely-
> assumption
>
> s.

This after (4)

a) noon's heat

can take full

possession
of your mind

b) and body'

s less deter

mining resour
ces that the a

wakening pro
cess become

c) s so impeded

that only an

additional
will-power

ed-urge can
reestablish

d) a semblance

of your own

self-identity
claim

s.

Einstein (3)

a) may have pro

ven that at ex

traordinary
speeds time

b) can be slow

ed–down but

in this in
tense Italian

ate heat it
seems as if

c) time has stopp

ed moving any

where's else
than perpetual

ly now.

That pier (2)

a) carried her

measured step

s beyond the de
termining hold

of her ground–

b) based thought

s in to the
watering

depths of un
requited silen

ces.

Reading-in-

the-pool with
one hand free

to absorb
that cleans

ing expectant–
message water–

purifying as
once in bibli

cal time
s.

One-sided (3)

a) ideological

poets with

their singul
ar self-deter

mining message

b) as if the o

ther-side-of-
the-street

could dilute
their pure-

blooded Span

c) ish or exact

ly 450 year
s later Ger

man–Aryan ac
ceptibil

ity.

For Corinne and S. L. *(3)*

a) Chopin'

s an imperfect–
fit whether

Polish or
French not a

single import

b) ant disciple

only the piano
itself ech

oing to this
day his finger

ing repertoire

c) of an especial

ly romantic
national

timely-evok
ing express

iveness.

Some poet (3)

a) s as Jaccottet

remain an

chored to a
self-suffi

b) cient even per

sonal sensibil

ity when gen
uinely sour

ced release

c) s most inti

mate wave
s of a time–

reflecting
relevance.

That self- *(2)*

a) appointed hotel

cat walking a

long a prede
termined route

of those un
evened curb–

b) stones of my

childhood

days balanc
ing-me-back

from what e
ver's left–

behind.

A little (2)

a) time-activat

ing girl with

blond bobbed
hair that

seemed almost
as a way of

b) keeping time

to the thres

hold of her
most particul

arly chosen–
presence.

Passing a (2)

a) long the shore

s of an histori

ical Italian
lake as if

time had been
flowing through

b) our receptive

but perhaps

less guided re
assuring remem

brance
s.

My momentary *(4)*

a) newly acquired

friend Benedict

and I exchang
ing hats His

b) then fashion

ably represent

ative whereas
mine about 4

sizes too small

c) and that age-

difference
of about 77

years matter
ed but little

d) as he in the

midst of his

own world-ex
ploring age.

His straight- *(3)*

a) ahead confident

ly self-reassur

ing manager
ial way Never

b) did he waver

from that ever–

successful
ly polished

air of a pro
minently in

c) spired past

promoting

even-more-like
ly future attain

ment
s.

Of Jewish *(3)*

a) descent many

of the saint

s and mystical
poets of ren

aissance Spain

b) suspected as

Christ should-
have-been from

an exiled peo
ple but here

and now as

c) Catholic as the

blood that
flowed through

His king
ly-invested

person.

A wind-be

> spoken morning
> neither here
>
> nor there blown
> into a con
>
> scious aware
> ness that to
>
> day's its very
> own person
>
> al time-tell
> ing.

These upstand (2)

> *a) ing waves recept*
>
> ively southward
>
> s inclining
> restlessly a
>
> wakened with a

> *b) secretly un*
>
> revealing but
> continuous
>
> ly express
> ive time-shar
>
> ing.

Lope de Vega' (3)

a) s daily express

ive world of

all that's
beautifying

b) (especially

such women)

signifying
his own need

to record its

c) here and now

nowheres-else
creative-spon

taneous re
solve.

Quevedo' (2)

a) s pre-Goyan

middle–down

ed his own
creative assur

ance of a
world (his own)

b) sick-at-its-

seams worn–

down decadent
but still artis

tically alive to
its most eter

nal splendor.

Some time

s as oft–time
s with Góngora

the language
stands–up to

its own need
for no–where

s–else but
mine.

That very-

little-blond-
eyed girl

s unsuccess
ful feeling

through to
that blue-

skied endeavoring
swing just

hanging there
so emptily

personed.

Lope or so *(3)*

a) it seems

through his

own say–so
daily called

b) by-Christ

(then a priest)

to abandon his
womanizing

ways but mañana
(tomorrow)

c) remained his

oft–consider

ed but sensu
ously denying–

resolve.

All-blond (2)

a) bleached or-

not pony–tail

ed to an arti
ficial same

ness that
they became as ex

b) changeable

as their e

qually pattern
ed dressed in

to a self–dis
guising demean

or.

Calderón *(3)*

a) Spain's great

est dramatist

and the last
(ing) voice of

its golden

b) age poetized

in "my love'
s confusion"

the "Lope
problem" a

c) truth so ex

actly observ

ed and yet un
equally if per

sonally answer
ed.

"To Christ-Cru *(3)*

a) cified" Miguel

de Guevara

its little
known but cer

b) tainly ascrib

ed author

so honestly
authentic

and most natur
ally voiced

c) that as a poet

and preacher

I could only
answer amen

amen.

Reading to (3)

a) Rosemarie and

to myself

two perspect
ives of the

b) same poem'

s otherwise

sensed and
seen as time

(we hope)
will realise

c) them accord

ing to its

own most
changeable

taste.

Few date *(3)*

a) s have become

so exactly and

intricately
timed as 1492

b) the unificat

ion of Spain

expulsion of
the Jews and

the discovery
of the New

c) World as if

a master-hand

had predeter
mined His own

fateful re
solved.

That folky

guitar-orient
ed modern Spain'

s classical
ly-otherwise

seems much ear
lier inhabit

ing its poetry'
s existential

raison d'être.

A good rest (4)

a) *aurant lives*

or dies be

cause of the
innovative

b) *qualities of*

the cook Where

as still–living–
poetry maintain

s its self–re

c) *taining path*

as with Shakes
peare because

it's linguisti
cally newly

d) *tracked to e*

ternal if time

ly repetitive–
truth

s.

In Nomine Domini
David Jaffin

Poetry books by David Jaffin

1. **Conformed to Stone,** Abelard-Schuman, New York 1968, London 1970.

2. **Emptied Spaces,** with an illustration by Jacques Lipschitz, Abelard-Schuman, London 1972.

3. **In the Glass of Winter,** Abelard-Schuman, London 1975, with an illustration by Mordechai Ardon.

4. **As One,** The Elizabeth Press, New Rochelle, N. Y. 1975.

5. **The Half of a Circle,** The Elizabeth Press, New Rochelle, N. Y. 1977.

6. **Space of,** The Elizabeth Press, New Rochelle, N. Y. 1978.

7. **Preceptions,** The Elizabeth Press, New Rochelle, N. Y. 1979.

8. **For the Finger's Want of Sound,** Shearsman, Plymouth, England 1982.

9. **The Density for Color,** Shearsman, Plymouth, England 1982.

10. **Selected Poems** with an illustration by Mordechai Ardon, English/Hebrew, Massada Publishers, Givatyim, Israel 1982.

11. **The Telling of Time,** Shearsman Books, Kentisbeare, England 2000 and Johannis, Lahr, Germany.

12. **That Sense for Meaning,** Shearsman Books, Kentisbeare, England 2001 and Johannis, Lahr, Germany.

13. **Into the timeless Deep,** Shearsman Books, Kentisbeare, England 2003 and Johannis, Lahr, Germany.

14. **A Birth in Seeing,** Shearsman Books, Exeter, England 2003 and Johannis, Lahr, Germany.

15. **Through Lost Silences,** Shearsman Books, Exeter, England 2003 and Johannis, Lahr, Germany.

16. **A voiced Awakening,** Shearsman Books, Exeter, England 2004 and Johannis, Lahr, Germany.

17. **These Time-Shifting Thoughts**, Shearsman Books, Exeter, England 2005 and Johannis, Lahr, Germany.

18. **Intimacies of Sound,** Shearsman Books, Exeter, England 2005 and Johannis, Lahr, Germany.

19. **Dream Flow** with an illustration by Charles Seliger, Shearsman Books, Exeter, England 2006 and Johannis, Lahr, Germany.

20. **Sunstreams** with an illustration by Charles Seliger, Shearsman Books, Exeter, England 2007 and Johannis, Lahr, Germany.

21. **Thought Colors,** with an illustration by Charles Seliger, Shearsman Books, Exeter, England 2008 and Johannis, Lahr, Germany.

22. **Eye-Sensing,** Ahadada, Tokyo, Japan and Toronto, Canada 2008.

23. **Wind-phrasings,** with an illustration by Charles Seliger, Shearsman Books, Exeter, England 2009 and Johannis, Lahr, Germany.

24. **Time shadows,** with an illustration by Charles Seliger, Shearsman Books, Exeter, England 2009 and Johannis, Lahr, Germany.

25. **A World mapped-out,** with an illustration by Charles Seliger, Shearsman Books, Exeter, England 2010.

26. **Light Paths,** with an illustration by Charles Seliger, Shearsman Books, Exeter, England 2011 and Edition Wortschatz, Schwarzenfeld, Germany.

27. **Always Now,** with an illustration by Charles Seliger, Shearsman Books, Bristol, England 2012 and Edition Wortschatz, Schwarzenfeld, Germany.

28. **Labyrinthed,** with an illustration by Charles Seliger, Shearsman Books, Bristol, England 2012 and Edition Wortschatz, Schwarzenfeld, Germany.

29. **The Other Side of Self,** with an illustration by Charles Seliger, Shearsman Books, Bristol, England 2012 and Edition Wortschatz, Schwarzenfeld, Germany.

30. **Light Sources,** with an illustration by Charles Seliger, Shearsman Books, Bristol, England 2013 and Edition Wortschatz, Schwarzenfeld, Germany.

31. **Landing Rights,** with an illustration by Charles Seliger, Shearsman Books, Bristol, England 2014 and Edition Wortschatz, Schwarzenfeld, Germany.

32. **Listening to Silence,** with an illustration by Charles Seliger, Shearsman Books, Bristol, England 2014 and Edition Wortschatz, Schwarzenfeld, Germany.

33. **Taking Leave,** with an illustration by Mei Fêng, Shearsman Books, Bristol, England 2014 and Edition Wortschatz, Schwarzenfeld, Germany.

34. **Jewel Sensed,** with an illustration by Paul Klee, Shearsman Books, Bristol, England 2015 and Edition Wortschatz, Schwarzenfeld, Germany.

35. **Shadowing Images**, with an illustration by Pieter de Hooch, Shearsman Books, Bristol, England 2015 and Edition Wortschatz, Schwarzenfeld.

36. **Untouched Silences**, with an illustration by Paul Seehaus, Shearsman Books, Bristol, England 2016 and Edition Wortschatz, Schwarzenfeld.

37. **Soundlesss Impressions**, with an illustration by Qi Baishi, Shearsman Books, Bristol, England 2016 and Edition Wortschatz, Schwarzenfeld.

38. **Moon Flowers**, with a photograph by Hannelore Bäumler, Shearsman Books, Bristol, England 2017 and Edition Wortschatz, Schwarzenfeld.

39. **The Healing of a Broken World**, with a photograph by Hannelore Bäumler, Shearsman Books, Bristol, England 2018 and Edition Wortschatz, Cuxhaven.

40. **Opus 40**, with a photograph by Hannelore Bäumler, Shearsman Books, Bristol, England 2018 and Edition Wortschatz, Cuxhaven.

41. **Identity Cause**, with a photograph by Hannelore Bäumler, Shearsman Books, Bristol, England 2018 and Edition Wortschatz, Cuxhaven.

42. **Kaleidoscope**, with a photograph by Hannelore Bäumler, Shearsman Books, Bristol, England 2019 and Edition Wortschatz, Cuxhaven.

43. **Snow-touched Imaginings**, with a photograph by Hannelore Bäumler, Shearsman Books, Bristol, England 2019 and Edition Wortschatz, Cuxhaven.

44. **Two-timed**, with a photograph by Hannelore Bäumler, Shearsman Books, Bristol, England 2020 and Edition Wortschatz, Cuxhaven.

45. **Corona Poems**, with a photograph by Hannelore Bäumler, Shearsman Books, Bristol, England 2020 and Edition Wortschatz, Cuxhaven.

46. **Spring Shadowings**, with a photograph by Hannelore Bäumler, Shearsman Books, Bristol, England 2021 and Edition Wortschatz, Cuxhaven.

47. **October: Cyprus Poems**, with an illustration by Odilon Redon, Shearsman Books, Bristol, England 2021 and Edition Wortschatz, Cuxhaven.

48. **Snow Dreams**, with a photograph by Hannelore Bäumler, Shearsman Books, Bristol, England 2022 and Edition Wortschatz, Cuxhaven.

49. **Ukraine Poems**, with a painting by Alfons Röllinger, Shearsman Books, Bristol, England 2022 and Edition Wortschatz, Cuxhaven.

50. **Simply Living Life**,with a photograph by
    Hannelore Bäumler, Shearsman Books, Bristol,
    England 2023 and Edition Wortschatz, Cuxhaven.

51. **Those 50 Lost Days and Nights**,with a
    photograph by Hannelore Bäumler, Shearsman
    Books, Bristol, England 2024 and Edition
    Wortschatz, Neudorf bei Luhe.

    Book on David Jaffin's poetry: Warren Fulton,
    Poemed on a beach, Ahadada, Tokyo, Japan and
    Toronto, Canada 2010.